christmas at home

Holiday DESSERTS

GAIL SATTLER

BARBOUR
PUBLISHING

ISBN 1-59310-040-X

Published by Barbour Publishing, Inc., P.O. Box 719, Uhrichsville, Ohio 44683, www.barbourbooks.com

Member of the
Evangelical Christian
Publishers Association

Printed in Canada.
5 4 3 2 1

contents

What better way to celebrate the joy of the Christmas season than to gather with friends and family!

Whether joined together for a meal, or simply coffee or tea and dessert, a sweet treat can enhance your time together.

To make your celebration with your loved ones even more special, here are some recipes for delicious Holiday Desserts *to share and enjoy.*

CAKES

But the angel said to her,

"Do not be afraid, Mary, you have found favor with God.

You will be with child and give birth to a son,

and you are to give him the name Jesus.

He will be great and will be called the Son of the Most High.

The Lord God will give him the throne of his father David,

and he will reign over the house of Jacob forever;

his kingdom will never end."

LUKE 1:30–33

Angel Food DESSERT CAKE—LEMON

1 angel food cake mix
1 pint vanilla ice cream

1 package lemon pie filling

Prepare cake mix as directed on package. Add 1 pint ice cream to hot lemon pie filling and whisk. Serve this sauce over slices of angel food cake and decorate with kiwi or other fruit.

Angel Food DESSERT CAKE—PINEAPPLE

1 package instant vanilla pudding
1 tin crushed pineapple

1 pint whipping cream
1 angel food cake, cut into 3 layers

Add instant pudding to crushed pineapple (with juice) and let stand for 10 minutes. Whip the cream and add the pudding/pineapple mixture. Put a generous amount of filling between layers and continue to ice top and sides of cake. Keep the cake refrigerated.

Cherry BUNDT CAKE

1 ¼ cups butter, softened
2 ¾ cups sugar
5 eggs
1 teaspoon almond extract
3 cups flour
1 teaspoon baking powder

¼ teaspoon salt
1 cup unsweetened evaporated milk
1 cup quartered maraschino
    cherries, well drained
Sifted icing sugar

Beat butter, sugar, eggs, and extract in large bowl on low speed of electric mixer until blended, then on high speed 5 minutes until light and fluffy. Combine flour, baking powder, and salt. Add dry ingredients alternately with evaporated milk to creamed mixture, mixing lightly after each addition. Fold in cherries. Turn batter into greased 12-cup Bundt or tube pan. Bake at 350° for 75–85 minutes. Cover with foil for last 10 minutes if becoming too brown. Cool in pan 10 minutes. Remove from pan. Cool completely. Dust with icing sugar before serving. A white icing drizzle is a pretty alternative decoration.

 Coffee CAKE

Topping:
- ⅓ cup brown sugar
- ⅓ cup sugar
- ¼ cup walnuts
- 1–1½ teaspoons cinnamon

Cake:
- ½ cup butter
- 1 cup sugar
- 2 eggs, beaten
- 1 teaspoon vanilla
- 1¼ cups sour cream
- 2 cups flour
- 2 teaspoons baking powder
- 1 teaspoon baking soda

Mix topping ingredients and set aside. Cream butter and sugar; add eggs and vanilla, then sour cream. Mix in dry ingredients. Place half of batter in a well-greased pan, then sprinkle on half the topping. Pour in remaining batter; top with rest of topping. Bake at 350° for 35–45 minutes.

Cranberry Orange COFFEE CAKE

Crumb Topping:
- ¾ cup flour
- ½ cup margarine
- ½ cup sugar

Cream Cheese Layer:
- ½ pound cream cheese, softened
- ⅓ cup sugar
- 1 egg
- 1 teaspoon vanilla extract

Cake:
- 2 cups flour
- 1 cup sugar
- 1½ teaspoons baking powder
- ½ teaspoon baking soda
- ½ teaspoon salt
- ¾ cup orange juice
- ¼ cup margarine
- 1 teaspoon vanilla extract
- 1 egg, beaten
- 2 cups coarsely chopped fresh or frozen cranberries
- 2 tablespoons grated orange rind

Crumb Topping: Stir together and set aside.

Cream Cheese Layer: Beat cream cheese and sugar until light and fluffy. Beat in egg and vanilla, set aside.

Cake: Combine dry ingredients. Stir in juice, margarine, vanilla, and egg. Fold in cranberries and orange rind just until mixed.

Pour into a 9-inch spring form pan. Spread cream cheese mixture over cake batter. Sprinkle with crumb topping. Bake at 350° for 65–70 minutes or until top springs back when lightly touched in center. Let cool on rack for 15 minutes. Remove outside ring and let cool completely. Makes 12 servings.

Cream Cheese APPLE CAKE

Pastry:

1¼ cups flour
⅓ cup sugar
½ cup margarine

1 egg yolk
¼ teaspoon vanilla

Mix flour with sugar. Cut in margarine. Beat egg yolk with vanilla. With fork, stir egg mixture into flour mixture. Press into bottom halfway up sides of a 9-inch spring form pan.

Topping:

4–5 apples (peeled, cored,
    quartered, and scored)
4 ounces cream cheese
¾ cup sugar

1 teaspoon vanilla
2 eggs
½ cup light cream
Nutmeg, to taste

Arrange apples on the pastry. Beat cream cheese until fluffy. Gradually beat sugar and vanilla. Add eggs one at a time, then light cream. Pour this mixture over the apples; sprinkle with nutmeg. Bake at 400° for 50–60 minutes. Serve warm or cool. Variation: Use blueberries instead of apples.

Fudge Ribbon CAKE

2 tablespoons butter
1 8-ounce package cream cheese
2¼ cups sugar
1 tablespoon cornstarch
3 eggs
1⅓ cups plus 2 tablespoons milk
1½ teaspoons vanilla

2 cups flour
1 teaspoon salt
1 teaspoon baking powder
½ teaspoon baking soda
½ cup butter, room temperature
3 squares unsweetened chocolate

Cream 2 tablespoons butter with cream cheese; add ¼ cup sugar and cornstarch. Add 1 egg, 2 tablespoons sugar, and cornstarch. Then add 1 egg, 2 tablespoons milk, and ½ teaspoon vanilla. Beat at high speed until smooth and creamy. Set aside. Grease and flour bottom of 13x9-inch pan. Combine flour with 2 cups sugar, salt, baking powder, and soda in large mixing bowl. Add ½ cup butter and 1 cup milk. Blend well at low speed. Add ⅓ cup milk, 2 eggs, chocolate, and 1 teaspoon vanilla, and continue beating 1½ minutes at low speed. Spread half of batter in pan. Spoon cheese mixture over batter. Top with remaining batter. Bake at 350° for 50–60 minutes. Cool and frost if desired.

Fruit Cocktail CAKE

1 cup flour
1 cup sugar
1 teaspoon baking soda
½ teaspoon salt
1 egg

1 15-ounce can fruit cocktail,
   drained
½ cup brown sugar
½ cup coconut

Mix flour, sugar, soda, and salt. Add beaten egg and drained fruit cocktail. Pour into ungreased 8-inch square pan. Mix brown sugar and coconut and spread over top. Bake at 350° for 30–35 minutes.

Gumdrop CAKE

1 cup dates
1 package raisins
1 cup butter
1/2 cup water
2 cups flour
2 eggs
1 teaspoon cinnamon

1 cup brown sugar
1 pound gumdrops,
   cut up (no black ones!)
1 cup sweetened applesauce
1 teaspoon baking soda
Nuts (optional)

Boil dates, raisins, butter, and water. Let cool. Add other ingredients. Bake at 350° for 1 1/2 hours.

Honey CAKE

1 cup brown sugar
5 eggs
1 cup creamed honey
1 cup oil

1 cup sour cream
2¾–3 cups flour
1¼ teaspoons baking powder
1¼ teaspoons baking soda

Beat sugar and eggs, add honey and beat well; add oil slowly, beating on lower speed until thoroughly blended. Add sour cream and beat. Combine flour, baking powder, and soda and add to mixture. Beat slowly until smooth. Pour into greased 9x12-inch pan. Bake for approximately 1 hour in a 350° oven.

Macaroon CAKE

Cake:

½ cup butter	1 cup flour
½ cup sugar	2 teaspoons baking powder
4 egg yolks	2 tablespoons milk

Cream butter and sugar; add egg yolks and beat. Sift flour and baking powder and add alternately with milk. Pour into 9x9-inch pan.

Meringue:

4 egg whites	½ cup sugar
Pinch of salt	1 cup coconut (unsweetened)

Beat egg whites with salt until peaks form. Add sugar and continue beating. Fold in coconut and spread on base. Bake at 325° for approximately 40 minutes.

Orange CAKE

4 eggs, separated
2 cups sugar
2 cups flour

1 tablespoon baking powder
2 cups orange juice, preferably
    freshly squeezed

Beat egg whites until stiff. Set aside. Beat egg yolks with sugar. Set aside. Sift together flour and baking powder; add to yolk mixture alternately with 1 cup orange juice, making three additions of dry and two of wet. Fold in egg whites. Pour into prepared cake pan. Bake in a floured 13x9-inch metal cake pan at 350° for 30 minutes or until toothpick inserted in center comes out clean. After removing cake from the oven, use a fork to pierce holes on top of the cake and pour remaining 1 cup orange juice on top. Cool cake in pan on wire rack.

Pineapple Dream CAKE

36 large marshmallows
1 cup milk
1 pint whipping cream

1 cup drained crushed pineapple
15 graham wafers

Melt marshmallows in milk. Whip cream, then fold in pineapple. Crush wafers and cover bottom of 9x9-inch pan (save some for sprinkling). Add marshmallow mixture to pineapple mixture. Pour into pan. Sprinkle remaining crushed wafers on top. Chill.

Queen Elizabeth CAKE

1 cup dates
1 cup hot water
1 teaspoon baking soda
¼ cup butter
1 cup sugar
1 egg
1½ cups flour

1 teaspoon baking powder
½ cup cream
1 teaspoon vanilla
6 teaspoons butter, melted
8 teaspoons brown sugar
4 teaspoons milk
1 cup shredded coconut

Cut up dates and pour hot water over dates with baking soda. Let cool. Mix 6 teaspoons butter, sugar, and egg, then add dry ingredients alternating with milk. Add dates and vanilla. Bake at 325° for 30 minutes. Beat together ¼ cup butter, brown sugar, and milk. Mix in coconut. Spread on cake and put back in oven for another 10 minutes.

Quick Cherry DESSERT

1 cup butter
1½ cups sugar
4 eggs
1 teaspoon almond extract
2 cups flour

2 tablespoons baking powder
1 21-ounce cherry pie filling
Powdered sugar to dust on top
Whipped cream to spread on top

Cream butter and sugar; add eggs, beat until light and fluffy. Add extract, stir in flour and baking powder; mix until smooth. Turn into buttered 13x9-inch pan. Spoon pie filling onto cake in 16 spots, spacing 4 across and 4 down evenly. Bake at 350° for 45–50 minutes or until done. Filling will sink into cake while baking. To serve, cut into 16 pieces. Place bottom side up on plate; dust with powdered sugar if desired and spoon whipped cream over each serving. Great served warm.

Sour Cream CHOCOLATE CHIP CAKE

6 tablespoons soft butter
1 cup sugar
2 eggs
1⅓ cups flour
1½ teaspoons baking powder
1 teaspoon baking soda

1 teaspoon cinnamon
1 cup sour cream
1 6-ounce package mini
    chocolate chips
1 tablespoon sugar

Mix butter and 1 cup sugar until blended. Beat in eggs one at a time. Stir baking powder, baking soda, and cinnamon into flour and blend with the creamed mixture. Mix in sour cream. Pour batter into a greased and floured 8x10-inch pan. Scatter the chocolate chips evenly over the batter. Then sprinkle 1 tablespoon sugar over top. Bake at 350° for 35 minutes or until cake just begins to pull away from sides of pan.

Raspberry Rainbow CAKE

1 package (2-layer size) white cake mix   1 tub Cool Whip
1 single package raspberry jelly powder

Prepare cake mix as directed on package using a well-greased and floured 13x9-inch pan and bake at 350° for 35 minutes. Cool in pan 15 minutes. Poke with fork at 1/2-inch intervals. (Do not remove from pan.) Prepare jelly powder as directed on package and pour over cake in pan. Chill 4 hours. Garnish with Cool Whip.

CHEESECAKES

At that time Mary got ready and hurried

to a town in the hill country of Judea,

where she entered Zechariah's home and greeted Elizabeth.

When Elizabeth heard Mary's greeting, the baby leaped in her womb,

and Elizabeth was filled with the Holy Spirit.

In a loud voice she exclaimed:

"Blessed are you among women, and blessed is the child you will bear!"

LUKE 1:39–42

 CHEESECAKE

1 cup flour   ½ cup sugar
½ cup butter   ¼ teaspoon vanilla

Mix until crumbly and press into bottom of greased 9-inch spring form pan.

2 8-ounce packages cream cheese   ½ cup sugar
2 eggs   1 teaspoon vanilla

Beat and pour over base.

4 cups sliced apples   5 teaspoons cinnamon
⅓ cup sugar   ¼ cup chopped pecans or almonds

Shake apples in a bag with sugar and cinnamon. Divide evenly on top of cheesecake. Top with nuts. Chill.

Blueberry CHEESECAKE

2 cups graham crumbs
1/4 cup butter, melted
1/2 cup sugar
1 8-ounce package cream
    cheese, softened

2 packages Dream Whip
2 cups blueberries, fresh or
    frozen (patted dry)

Mix crumbs and butter; press into 13x9-inch pan. Sprinkle sugar on blueberries; set aside. Whip together cream cheese and Dream Whip (prepared according to directions on package). Gently stir in blueberries; pour into crust. Chill.

Cherry Cheese SQUARES

2 cups graham wafer crumbs
3 tablespoons brown sugar
½ cup melted butter
1 8-ounce package cream
    cheese, softened

1 cup icing sugar
1½ cups whipped cream
1 can cherry pie filling

Mix crumbs, brown sugar, and melted butter. Save ½ cup and put the rest into 9-inch square buttered pan. Bake at 350° for 10 minutes; cool. Mix cream cheese and icing sugar, then blend in whipped cream. Spread half over cooled base. Spread cherry pie filling; then rest of mix. Sprinkle balance of crumbs on top. Refrigerate.

Cottage CHEESECAKE SQUARES

These squares are low in sugar and fat!

Crust:

1 cup graham cracker crumbs
3 tablespoons melted butter

1 teaspoon cinnamon

Filling:

1¼ pounds solid curd (pressed)
  cottage cheese
½ cup sugar

2 eggs
1 teaspoon vanilla

Topping:

1 cup unflavored yogurt
2 tablespoons sugar

¼ teaspoon vanilla
12 strawberries, halved,
  fresh or frozen

To make crust: Mix all 3 ingredients and press firmly into 8x8-inch pan.

To make filling: Beat cottage cheese and sugar until smooth, or blend in food processor blender. Add eggs, one at a time, and beat in vanilla. Pour over crust and bake at 350° for 25–30 minutes or until filling begins to puff slightly. Do not allow to brown. Remove from oven and let rest for 5 minutes.

To make topping: Combine yogurt, sugar, and vanilla. Spoon evenly over cheesecake. Return to oven for 5 minutes. Allow to cool to room temperature, then refrigerate overnight. Cut into 24 squares and top each piece with a strawberry half. Serve chilled.

Chocolate Chip CHEESECAKE

1½ cups finely crushed Oreo cookies
3 tablespoons butter, melted
3 small packages cream
   cheese, softened
1 can Eagle sweetened
   condensed milk

2 teaspoons vanilla
3 eggs
1 cup semisweet chocolate
   chips, divided
1 teaspoon flour

Combine Oreo crumbs and butter; press into 9-inch spring form pan. Beat cream cheese until fluffy, then beat in milk, vanilla, and eggs. Toss ½ cup chocolate chips with flour to coat; stir into cheese mixture. Pour into prepared pan and sprinkle with remaining chips. Bake for 1 hour at 300° or until cake springs back when lightly touched. Cool. Chill. Serve.

Fruit Cocktail CHEESECAKE

1 package chocolate grahams, crushed
2½ tablespoons butter
2 small packages cream cheese

2 tablespoons sugar
1 can drained fruit cocktail
2 packages Dream Whip,
    prepared using package directions

Mix crumbs and butter and press into 9x9-inch pan. Be sure to save some crumbs to sprinkle on top of cheesecake. Mix together softened cream cheese, sugar, and fruit cocktail. Fold in prepared Dream Whip. Pour over crumbs. Sprinkle saved crumbs on top. Chill and serve.

Orange CHEESECAKE

1 3-ounce package orange jelly powder
1 ½ cups graham crumbs
¼ cup butter
2 envelopes gelatin
½ cup cold water
½ cup milk
1 cup sugar

2 egg yolks
1 8-ounce package cream cheese
2 packages Dream Whip
2 egg whites
1 teaspoon vanilla
2 cans mandarin oranges, drained

Make jelly powder according to package directions; refrigerate until almost set. Combine crumbs and butter; press into 9x13-inch or free-form pan. Soak gelatin in ½ cup cold water; let stand. Combine milk, sugar, egg yolks, and mix well. Cook until thick, then add gelatin. Cool completely. Cream cheese until fluffy, add to gelatin mix. Beat Dream Whip, then beat egg whites until firm. Fold together, adding vanilla. Gently add drained orange pieces. Pour in pan over crust. Beat jelly until frothy, put on top. Refrigerate for 1 day before serving.

Peach DELIGHT

Base:
1¼ cups graham crumbs

¼ cup sugar

⅓ cup melted butter

Filling:
12 ounces softened cream cheese

½ cup sugar

Almond extract to taste

Topping:
2 cups peach pie filling (or your choice)

3 tablespoons softened butter

½ cup flour

½ cup sliced almonds

¼ cup brown sugar

Mix base and press into 9x13-inch pan. Bake at 375° for 8 minutes. Chill 1 hour in fridge. Mix filling and spread on base. Spread pie filling on top of this mixture. Combine flour, sugar, and butter. Mix well. Stir in almonds. Sprinkle over fruit filling. Bake at 375° for 25–30 minutes or until golden brown. When cooled completely, cut into 15 squares and top each square with ½ peach.

Pistachio CHEESECAKE

For variation, try using chocolate pudding.

Base:

    ¹/₂ cup butter or margarine   1 cup flour
    3 tablespoons icing sugar

Mix together; press into an 8x13-inch pan. Bake at 325° for 15–20 minutes; cool.

Filling:

    ²/₃ cup icing sugar   1 8-ounce package cream cheese,
    ¹/₂ tub large Cool Whip   softened

Whip and spread on cooled base.

Topping:
2 packages pistachio (or chocolate) instant pudding
2½ cups milk

Whip until slightly thick; pour over filling. Top with other half Cool Whip and refrigerate.

Magic Cherry CHIFFON CHEESECAKE

1 unbaked 9-inch pie shell (or
  1 9-inch graham cracker
  crumb crust)
1 small package cream
  cheese, softened
½ can Eagle Brand sweetened
  condensed milk

2 eggs, separated
2 tablespoons lemon juice
Pinch salt
1 can cherry pie filling

Bake pie shell according to package instructions. While crust is cooling, prepare filling. Beat cream cheese until fluffy. Add condensed milk and egg yolks and beat until smooth. Stir in lemon juice. Beat egg whites with salt to soft peaks. Fold into mixture. Pour into baked pie shell. Bake at 300° for 30 minutes or until cake springs back when lightly touched. Chill and top with cherry pie filling. For a variation: top with blueberry pie filling.

EAT WITH A SPOON!

So Joseph also went up from the town of Nazareth in Galilee to Judea,

to Bethlehem the town of David,

because he belonged to the house and line of David.

While they were there, the time came for the baby to be born,

and she gave birth to her firstborn, a son.

She wrapped him in cloths and placed him in a manger,

because there was no room for them in the inn.

LUKE 2:4, 6–7

Broken Glass DESSERT

Base:

    1 ½ cups graham wafer crumbs
    ⅓ cup sugar
    ⅓ cup butter, melted
    1 teaspoon cinnamon

Filling:

1 3-ounce package red jelly powder	½ cup sugar
1 3-ounce package lime jelly powder	1 envelope unflavored gelatin
1 3-ounce package lemon jelly powder	½ cup cold water
4 ½ cups hot water, divided	½ cup hot water
2 ½ cups whipping cream	¼ cup pineapple juice

Mix together ingredients for base. Press into 13x9-inch pan and chill. Dissolve each jelly powder in 1½ cups hot water. Pour into separate pans; chill and cut into ½-inch cubes. Whip cream; add sugar. Soften gelatin in the ½ cup cold water; dissolve in hot water and add pineapple juice. When cool, combine with whipped cream mixture. Add whipped cream/gelatin mix to jelly cubes. Pour into chilled crust. Chill. Makes 12 or more servings.

Baked Lemon SPONGE PUDDING

2 medium eggs, separated
2 tablespoons butter or margarine
3/4 cup sugar
3 tablespoons flour

1 tablespoon grated lemon rind
1/4 cup fresh lemon juice
Pinch salt
1 1/2 cups milk

Beat egg whites and set aside. Cream butter and sugar together. Add egg yolks and beat well. Stir in everything else except the egg whites and mix well. Fold beaten egg whites into mixture and pour into buttered 1 1/2-quart baking dish and place in pan of hot water. Bake at 350° for 45 minutes. Makes 4 to 6 servings.

Black Forest TRIFLE

1 package Fudge Cake
1 large package instant
    chocolate pudding
1 quart cherry pie filling

¾ quart whipping cream
Chocolate curls
Maraschino cherries

Prepare and bake Fudge Cake in 2 layers, then slice into chunks. Prepare chocolate pudding. In a large bowl, layer chunks of chocolate cake, pudding, pie filling, and whipping cream—making 3 repetitions and ending with a layer of cake and cream. Garnish with whipping cream, chocolate curls, and cherries. Chill and serve.

Caramel RAISIN PUDDING

1 ½ cups boiling water   ½ cup brown sugar
2 teaspoons butter   ¼ teaspoon vanilla

Combine and boil for 5 minutes. Pour hot syrup into buttered baking dish.
Set aside.

½ cup seedless raisins   1 teaspoon baking powder
¼ cup milk   ¼ teaspoon salt
¾ cup flour   2 teaspoons butter

Soak raisins in water for 5 minutes. Drain; stir in milk. Combine flour,
baking powder, salt, and butter. Add raisins and milk. Drop batter from spoon
over hot sauce. Bake at 350° for 25–30 minutes. Serve warm.

Chocolate DELIGHT

1 package (4 serving size) instant chocolate pudding
2 cups milk
2 cups Cool Whip, thawed
Chocolate garnish (chocolate chips, grated chocolate, chocolate cookie
　　crumbs, or garnish with strawberries instead)

Prepare pudding with milk as directed on package. Fold 1½ cups Cool
Whip topping into pudding; spoon into 4 dessert dishes. Top with remaining
½ cup Cool Whip and chocolate garnish.

Chocolate Ripple ORANGE CAKE

1 cup soft butter or margarine
1 cup sugar
3 large eggs
1 cup sour cream

1 3/4 cups flour
1 teaspoon baking powder
1 teaspoon baking soda
1 whole grated orange rind

Cream butter and sugar until light and fluffy. Add eggs; beat 1 minute at low speed. Blend in sour cream. Add dry ingredients and rind and blend thoroughly. Spoon 1/4 cake batter into greased and floured 10-inch tube pan.

Alternate layers with:

    ½ cup sugar   1 heaping tablespoon cocoa
    3 tablespoons cinnamon

Bake at 325° for 60 minutes. Cool 10 minutes and invert.

While cooling, mix:

    ¼ cup orange juice
    ⅓ cup icing sugar

Boil for a few minutes and drizzle over cake.

Chocolate Strawberry MOUSSE DELIGHT

Chocolate Base:

- ½ cup shortening
- 3 squares unsweetened chocolate
- 1¼ cups sugar
- 1 teaspoon vanilla
- 3 eggs
- ⅔ cup flour
- ½ teaspoon baking powder
- ¼ teaspoon salt

Melt shortening and chocolate in pan on low heat, stirring until smooth. Remove from heat. Add sugar, vanilla, and eggs. Mix well. Combine flour, baking powder, and salt. Add to chocolate mixture and stir until well blended. Spread into a greased 9-inch spring form pan. Bake at 350° for 25–30 minutes.

Topping:

1 package frozen sliced strawberries
with syrup
1 pouch gelatin
½ cup sugar

2 tablespoons lemon juice
2 cups whipping cream
Fresh strawberries for garnish,
if desired

Drain strawberries and reserve liquid. Add water to make 1¼ cups of liquid. Combine gelatin and sugar in pan. Stir in strawberry liquid and lemon juice. Bring to boil. Stir constantly to dissolve sugar and gelatin. Remove from heat and chill until starting to set. Beat 1¼ cups of the whipping cream to stiff peaks. Beat gelatin mix with electric mixer until light. Fold into whipped cream. Fold in drained strawberries. Spread evenly over base in pan and chill until set, approx 1 ½ hours or overnight. To serve, beat remaining whipping cream to stiff peaks and garnish with fresh strawberries if desired.

Chocolate TRIFLE

1 chocolate cake mix, and ingredients
1 cup cold coffee
6 Skor chocolate bars
1 instant chocolate pudding mix
1 small tub Cool Whip

Make 1 chocolate cake mix according to directions. Bake. Cut into chunks and sprinkle coffee over top. Break up chocolate bars into fine pieces. Make chocolate pudding according to directions; add half the Skor pieces, then add to cake pieces. Top with Cool Whip, then top with the rest of the Skor pieces.

Cranberry STORM

1 cup graham crumbs
1/4 cup butter, melted
1 small package cranberry jelly powder
1/2 cup whole cranberry sauce
Rind of 1 orange
Peeled sections of 1 orange
1 tub (4 cups) thawed Cool Whip

Mix crumbs and butter into 9-inch square pan; set aside. Mix jelly powder with 2/3 cup boiling water, then 1 cup cold water. Stir in cranberry sauce, orange rind, and orange sections. Fold in Cool Whip. Chill until slightly thickened, about 10 minutes. Spoon into crust. Freezes well.

FROZEN *Peanut Butter* MOUSSE

1 egg white
1/4 cup sugar
1 cup heavy cream
1/2 cup creamy peanut butter
1/2 cup milk

1/4 cup light corn syrup
Dash salt
Spray-type whipped cream
4 maraschino cherries, with stems

Beat egg white into soft peaks, then add sugar and beat into stiff peaks. Set aside. Beat cream until stiff; set aside. Beat peanut butter and milk until smooth. Mix in corn syrup and salt until well blended. Fold egg white mixture and cream mixture into peanut butter mixture until smooth and well blended. Pour into eight 4-ounce serving cups or one 1-quart bowl. Cover and freeze until firm, about 1 hour for small cups, 3 hours for single container. To serve, remove from freezer and let stand in fridge for 10 minutes (30 minutes for single container). Garnish with spray-style whipped cream and maraschino cherry.

 CAKE

40 graham wafers, crushed
8 tablespoons butter
2 packages jelly powder, any flavor
1 cup hot water

1 cup sugar
Juice from 1 lemon
2 cans sweetened evaporated
milk, chilled

Mix crumbs and butter; place 3 tablespoons aside for top. Spread balance over 9x12-inch pan. Dissolve jelly powder in hot water. Add sugar and lemon juice. Cool. Whip evaporated milk (which has been well chilled) until creamy. Add jelly powder mixture and beat until well mixed. Spread with remaining crumbs. Set in fridge.

Lemon Cream DESSERT

½ cup butter
1 package vanilla wafers, crushed
1 6-ounce frozen lemonade concentrate, thawed
1 can Eagle Brand milk
1 pint whipping cream, whipped

Melt butter; add crushed vanilla wafers. Press into 9x9-pan. Save some for topping. Chill. Mix lemonade, milk, and whipped cream. Spread over base; sprinkle with reserved crumbs. Refrigerate 24 hours before serving.

Marshmallow CHERRY DESSERT

Base:

2 cups crushed graham wafers   ½ cup melted butter
6 tablespoons icing sugar

Combine and line a 9x12-inch pan, reserving 2 tablespoons for sprinkling on top.

Filling:

2 small cartons whipping cream   1 can cherry pie filling
1 package mini marshmallows

Whip the cream and fold in marshmallows. Put ½ onto base. Cover with pie filling and top with remaining whipped cream mixture. Top with reserved crumbs. Set in fridge for two days prior to serving.

Orange PUDDING

Juice:

3 oranges (juice from 3, rind from 1)
¾ cup boiling water

¾ cup sugar
1 tablespoon butter

Mix together and boil for 8 minutes.

Batter:

⅔ cup sugar
1 tablespoon butter
Pinch salt

½ cup milk
¾ cup flour
1 teaspoon baking powder

Mix all batter ingredients. Put batter over juice and bake at 350° for 30 minutes. Serve with whipped cream or ice cream.

Pineapple SUPREME

2 cups graham cracker crumbs
⅓ cup butter or margarine
1 large container sour cream
2 large cans crushed pineapple
2 4-ounce packages vanilla instant pudding

Mix crumbs and butter and press into bottom of 13x9-inch pan. Mix remaining ingredients and pour over graham wafer crust. Chill until set.

Very Easy TRIFLE

1 package strawberry jelly powder
3 tablespoons custard powder
3 tablespoons sugar
2½ cups milk
1 angel food cake, made according
   to package directions

1 can fruit cocktail, drained
1 package strawberries, drained
1 pint whipping cream, whipped

Prepare jelly powder according to package directions, reducing water by $\frac{1}{2}$ cup. Cool and set. Cut into 1-inch cubes. Set aside. Mix custard powder and sugar. Gradually add milk and cook, stirring over medium heat. When it comes to a boil, remove from heat; set aside to cool. Cut angel food cake into 1-inch squares. Set aside. Drain fruit cocktail and strawberries. Pat dry with a paper towel. Set aside. Layer as follows 3 times: (1) cake pieces, (2) custard, (3) jelly squares, (4) fruit, (5) whipped cream. After third repetition, garnish with a few strawberries. Chill. Serve.

Pistachio REFRIGERATOR DESSERT

40 Ritz crackers, crushed
  (or chocolate wafers)
½ cup butter or margarine
2 boxes pistachio instant pudding
1½ cups milk

4 cups vanilla ice cream
Whipping cream or any
  dessert topping
Nuts (optional)
Chocolate shavings (optional)

Mix crumbs and butter and pat into a 9x13-inch pan. Bake at 350° for 10 minutes; cool. Mix pistachio pudding with milk and ice cream. Blend well. Spread on baked base. Top with whipped topping and garnish with nuts or shaved chocolate. Place in freezer. To serve, let sit at room temperature for approximately 30 minutes.

Raspberry CREAM CAKE

1 package raspberry jelly powder
½ cup boiling water

6 large ice cubes
1 cup whipping cream

Put jelly powder and water in blender on high for 15 seconds. Add ice and blend on high until the ice is gone. Pour in whipping cream and blend for a few seconds. Pour into individual serving dishes. Chill.

Whip 'n Chill STRAWBERRY DESSERT

1 cup graham crumbs
$\frac{1}{3}$ cup butter
1 package strawberry Whip 'n Chill

1 package frozen strawberries,
    not drained
1 package strawberry jelly powder

Combine crumbs and butter to make a crust; press into bottom of 9x9-inch pan. Over this, spread Whip 'n Chill. Let set 1 hour in fridge. Heat liquid from frozen strawberries, adding jelly powder to this instead of water. Cool and pour over Whip 'n Chill. Put in fridge to set. Top with whipped cream.

FRUITCAKES & FRUIT BREADS

"Do not be afraid. I bring you good news of great joy
that will be for all the people.
Today in the town of David a Savior has been born to you;
he is Christ the Lord. This will be a sign to you:
You will find a baby wrapped in cloths and lying in a manger."

LUKE 2:10–12

Classic Christmas FRUITCAKE

1 pound dark raisins
1 pound mixed fruit
3 pineapple rings
2 pounds sultana raisins
1 pound glazed cherries
1 pound mixed peel
1 pound blanched almonds
3½ cups flour
1 pound butter
1 pound sugar

12 eggs
1 teaspoon baking soda
2 ounces unsweetened chocolate
1 cup grape jelly
1 teaspoon salt
1 teaspoon nutmeg
1 teaspoon cloves
1 teaspoon allspice
2 tablespoons cinnamon

Pour boiling water on raisins and let sit for a few minutes. Drain and dry. Cover fruits and almonds with 1 cup of flour. Mix well. Cream butter and sugar, add eggs one at a time and beat. Add melted chocolate and softened jelly. Sift together remaining flour, soda, salt, and spices. Add to fruit and mix well. Put 2 layers of brown paper (greased) in loaf tins and pour in batter. Bake at 275° for 4–5 hours. For smaller loaf pans, bake for only 2½ hours. Cool 5 minutes and remove from pans.

Christmas BREAD

1 loaf frozen white bread dough, thawed
½ cup mixed candied fruit
¼ cup chopped or sliced almonds
Soft butter or margarine

2 tablespoons sugar
½ teaspoon cinnamon
Vanilla icing (optional)

Let dough rise until doubled in size. Roll out on floured surface into 14x7-inch rectangle. Sprinkle half with fruit and almonds. Fold uncovered dough over fruits; roll out again. Shape into round ball. Place into greased 9-inch round pan. Brush top with butter. Sprinkle cinnamon sugar mixture over top. Cover; let rise in warm place until doubled in size, about 1 to 1½ hours. Bake at 350° until golden brown, about 30–35 minutes. Frost with vanilla icing and decorate with additional candied fruit and almond slices, if desired.

Jewelled FRUITCAKE

¾ cup flour
¾ cup sugar
½ teaspoon baking powder
½ teaspoon salt
3 eggs, beaten
1½ teaspoons vanilla
1 8-ounce package (2 cups) dried apricots

1 8-ounce package (1½ cups) pitted dates
1 cup drained green maraschino cherries
1 cup drained red maraschino cherries
1 cup candied pineapple, cut up
¾ pound whole Brazil nuts

Mix dry ingredients with eggs and vanilla. Add fruit and nuts. Spread evenly in 2 loaf tins lined with greased aluminum foil. Bake at 275° for 1¾ hours or until toothpick comes out clean when you poke it. If necessary, cover with foil the last 30 minutes of cooking to prevent overbrowning. Remove from pans and cool. Wrap in plastic or aluminum foil. Store in cool place.

Mount Vernon RAISIN FRUITCAKE

2 cups sultana raisins
1 cup glacé cherries, halved
2 cups candied pineapple, diced
Orange juice (enough to cover fruit)
1 cup butter
2 cups sugar

5 eggs, well beaten
3 cups flour
1½ teaspoons baking powder
1 teaspoon salt
2 cups pecans

Combine the first three fruits with juice; mix well. Cover and set aside overnight. Next day, cream butter; add sugar and beat until light and fluffy. Then add beaten eggs and blend mixture together. Sift flour, baking powder, and salt together and stir into batter. Pour this batter over fruit mixture and stir in the pecans. Mix until fruits are well blended. Pour batter into foil or parchment paper lined 10- or 11-inch tube pan. Bake at 300° for 2½–3 hours, or until a cake tester inserted in the center comes out clean. Cool cake for ½ hour, then remove foil or paper and let cake cool. When thoroughly cool, wrap cake in foil and allow cake to ripen for at least three weeks before serving.

Norwegian HOLIDAY BREAD

½ cup butter
½ cup milk
1 package dry yeast
½ cup warm water
¼ cup sugar
1 teaspoon salt
1 cup raisins

½ cup chopped candied
    cherries (red and green)
½ cup almonds
1 egg, slightly beaten
3½ to 4 cups flour
Icing sugar

Heat butter and milk until butter is melted; cool to lukewarm. Soften yeast in warm water. Stir in sugar, salt, raisins, cherries, and nuts. Mix egg into cooled milk mixture. Add flour to form a stiff dough, beating well after each addition. Let rise in warm place until doubled in bulk, 1½ to 2 hours. Turn on floured board. Toss lightly until coated with flour and not sticky. Divide dough into 2 parts and shape into round loaves. Place on greased baking sheets or 2 well-greased 8-inch round pans. Divide dough into 3 parts; shape dough into round loaves and place in 3 well-greased coffee tins. Let rise until doubled in bulk. Bake at 350° for 30–35 minutes. If desired, glaze with icing sugar mixed with just enough water to make a nice glaze.

White FRUITCAKE

3 cups mixed candied fruit
2 cups gold raisins
1½ cups candied pineapple
1½ cups glazed cherries
1½ cups almonds, chopped
1 cup glazed mixed peel
2 cups flour
2 teaspoon baking powder

½ teaspoon salt
½ cup softened butter
1 cup sugar
3 eggs
1 tablespoon coarsely grated
    orange rind
1 teaspoon almond flavoring
½ cup orange juice

Line 2 loaf pans with greased waxed paper. Combine fruits and almonds. Toss with ½ cup of the flour and set aside. Mix dry ingredients and set aside. Cream butter and sugar until fluffy. Beat in eggs one at a time; add rind and flavoring, and beat again. Stir in flour mix alternately with juice until combined. Fold in fruit and pour into pans. Bake at 250° for 2½ hours with a pan of water or until done. Cool completely before removing from pans.

Nut BREAD

4 cups flour
4 teaspoons baking powder
½ teaspoon salt
1 cup brown sugar

1 cup walnuts
1 egg
2 cups milk
1 teaspoon melted butter

Sift flour, baking powder, and salt together. Add brown sugar and nuts. Beat egg and mix with milk, then stir into dry mixture. Beat in melted butter and put into bread pan. Let rise for 20 minutes. Bake in 250° oven for 30 minutes or until golden.

Layered Desserts

When they had seen him,
they spread the word concerning what had been
told them about this child,
and all who heard it were amazed at what
the shepherds said to them.

Luke 2:17–18

Apple SURPRISE

1 cup flour
1 teaspoon sugar
1/8 teaspoon salt
2 teaspoons baking powder
1/2 cup milk
1 cup chopped apple

1 cup brown sugar
1 tablespoon lemon juice
1 1/2 cups boiling water
2 tablespoons butter
1/2 teaspoon cinnamon

Mix dry ingredients, add milk, then work in chopped apple. Spread this mixture evenly in the bottom of a greased baking dish. Blend brown sugar, lemon juice, boiling water, and butter. Pour over batter. Sprinkle cinnamon on top. Bake at 375° for 20–25 minutes. When done the sauce will be bubbling underneath.

Cherries JUBILEE

Mixture 1:

2 cups graham wafer crumbs
(¼ set aside)

⅓ cup butter or margarine
1 can cherry pie filling

Mixture 2:

½ pint whipping cream, whipped

1 package mini marshmallows

To assemble:

Put all of Mixture 1 in 13x9-inch pan. Cover with half can of cherry pie filling. Put half of Mixture 2 on top of filling. Cover with the rest of the cherry pie filling. Use the second half of Mixture 2. Top with remaining crumbs. Chill and serve.

Cool Christmas STRIPES

1 4-ounce package green jelly powder
1 package Knox gelatin
½ cup cold water
¾ cup sugar
1 cup whipping cream

1 cup sour cream
1 teaspoon vanilla
1 4-ounce package red jelly powder
1 cup boiling water
1 15-ounce can blueberries with juice

Can be made in a large bowl, or individual clear dessert/parfait glasses.

First layer: Prepare green jelly powder according to directions on box. Place in large bowl or in individual clear serving glasses (each ⅓ full).

Second layer: Mix gelatin with ½ cup cold water in saucepan. Heat to dissolve but do not boil. Add sugar. Cool. Whip cream and mix with sour cream and vanilla. Mix with the gelatin mixture; pour over first layer.

Third layer: Dissolve red jelly powder with 1 cup boiling water (not according to directions). Add can of blueberries and the juice and pour over the second layer. Let stand in fridge for several hours before serving.

 *Fluffy* LAYERED JELLY CAKE

2 cups graham crumbs
⅓ cup butter or margarine
2 packages red jelly powder
1 small can evaporated milk
3 packages green jelly powder
2 packages orange jelly powder

2 packages blue (or dark color)
   jelly powder
½ cup cold milk
½ teaspoon vanilla
1 package Dream Whip

Bottom: Mix crumbs and butter; press into 9x13-inch pan.

1st layer: Mix 2 red jelly powders with 1 cup boiling water; add 2 cups cold water. When partially set, whip evaporated milk and beat with jelly powder. Pour over bottom.

2nd layer: Mix 3 packages green jelly powder with 1 cup boiling water; add 2 cups cold water. When almost set, pour over first layer.

3rd layer: Mix 2 packages orange jelly powder with 1 cup boiling water; add 1 cup cold water. When almost set, whip until fluffy (just whipped jelly powder, no extras). Pour over second layer.

4th layer: Mix 2 packages blue jelly powder with ½ cup boiling water. Set until firm; slice into squares. Using milk and vanilla, mix Dream Whip according to package instructions; fold in jelly powder squares, then spread over third layer.

Creamy JELLY LAYERS

1 small package jelly powder (lime, cherry, or any dark color)
1½ cups boiling water
2 cups frozen Cool Whip (reserve remainder of container for topping)

Dissolve jelly powder in boiling water. When jelly powder is dissolved, immediately whisk in frozen Cool Whip and pour into individual see-through serving containers. Chill until set. This separates into 2 layers. When set, top with unused thawed Cool Whip (must be set enough so the Cool Whip will not sink). Serves 4.

Rainbow RIBBONS

Takes a long time to prepare, but it's worth it!

5 single packages jelly powder, any colors   1 cup plain or vanilla yogurt
6¼ cups boiling water

Dissolve 1 package jelly powder in 1¼ cups water. Pour ¾ cup of this mixture into an 8-cup ring mold. Chill until set but not firm, about 15 minutes. At the same time, chill remaining jelly in bowl until slightly thickened. Gradually blend in 3 tablespoons yogurt. Pour over jelly in mold. Note: Instead of pouring onto the jelly, pour onto a spoon to "splash" it on. Chill until set but not firm, about 15 minutes. Repeat with remaining jelly, making layers. When assembled, chill until firm, about 2 hours. To unmold, dip mold into warm water for 10 seconds. Place serving plate on top of mold; invert onto plate.

Vinatorte

Filling:

1 pound prunes, boiled, stoned,
    and put through chopper
½ cup of water from boiling prunes

1 teaspoon cinnamon
¾ cup sugar
1 teaspoon vanilla

Pastry:

1 cup butter
1 cup sugar
2 eggs
1 teaspoon baking powder

4–5 cups flour
1 tablespoon almond extract
3 tablespoons cream

Combine all filling ingredients; bring to a boil and cook a few minutes, then add vanilla. Set aside. Cream butter and sugar; add eggs one at a time. Sift dry ingredients and work in. Add flavoring and cream. Knead in all the flour and divide into nine parts. Put each into 9-inch pans and bake at 375° until golden brown. Remove from pan while hot. Set until cool. Begin with pastry; layer with filling, ending with pastry. Wrap in foil and let cure for 3–4 weeks.

LOAVES

Now there was a man in Jerusalem called Simeon,
who was righteous and devout.
He was waiting for the consolation of Israel,
and the Holy Spirit was upon him.
It had been revealed to him by the Holy Spirit that he would
not die before he had seen the Lord's Christ. Moved by the Spirit,
he went into the temple courts.
When the parents brought in the child Jesus to do for him what
the custom of the Law required,
Simeon took him in his arms and praised God.

LUKE 2:25–28

Banana POUND CAKE

1 package yellow cake mix
⅓ cup salad oil
1⅓ cups mashed banana
  (approximately 3)
1 package instant vanilla pudding

4 eggs at room temperature
½ cup water
½ teaspoon cinnamon
½ teaspoon nutmeg
Confectioners' sugar

Combine all ingredients and beat for 4 minutes. Pour into 10-inch tube pan (greased) and bake for 1 hour at 325°. Dust with confectioners' sugar before serving.

Blueberry Orange LOAF

½ teaspoon baking soda
2 teaspoons baking powder
2 cups flour
¾ cup sugar
¼ teaspoon salt
1 tablespoon grated orange rind
¼ cup orange juice

¼ cup butter, melted
¾ cup milk
1 egg, beaten
1 cup fresh or frozen blueberries,
    drained and dried
½ cup chopped nuts

Sift first five ingredients (dry ingredients) into a bowl. Combine the next five ingredients and stir into the flour mixture. Beat well. Grease a 9x5x3-inch loaf pan and spread with one-third batter. Sprinkle with half the blueberries and nuts. Add another third of batter and remaining fruit and nuts. Add remaining batter. Bake at 350° for approximately 50 minutes.

Cherry POUND CAKE

³/₄ pound butter
1 ½ cups sugar
6 eggs
1 teaspoon vanilla

3 cups flour
½ teaspoon salt
1 teaspoon baking powder
1 cup candied cherries, halved

Cream butter and sugar; add beaten egg yolks and vanilla. Stir in dry ingredients with cherries. Gently fold in stiffly beaten egg whites. Bake at 325° for 1 hour 45 minutes.

Cinnamon Swirl LOAF

1 cup sour cream
1 teaspoon baking soda
½ cup butter
1 cup sugar
2 eggs

1 teaspoon vanilla
1¾ cups flour
1 teaspoon baking powder
½ cup brown sugar
1½ tablespoons cinnamon

Mix sour cream and baking soda together and allow to stand while mixing rest of loaf. Blend butter, sugar, eggs, and vanilla together. Beat until fluffy. Mix flour and baking powder together. Add flour mixture to butter mixture alternately with sour cream. In a separate bowl, mix the brown sugar and cinnamon. Put one-third of the batter into a greased 9x5x3-loaf pan; spread cinnamon mixture and repeat to form layers. Then swirl with a knife. Bake for approximately 1 hour at 350°.

Cranberry Orange LOAF

¼ cup butter or margarine
1 cup sugar
1 egg
Juice of 1 orange
   (water to make ¾ cup)
2 cups flour

1½ teaspoons baking powder
½ teaspoon baking soda
½ teaspoon salt
1½ cups frozen or fresh cranberries
Grated rind of 1 orange
½ cup chopped pecans or walnuts

Combine butter, sugar, and egg. Beat until smooth, stir in juice. Combine dry ingredients and fruit, rind, and nuts, and add to butter mixture, stirring just until moistened. Scrape into 9x5x3-inch loaf pan. Bake at 350° for 1 hour. Test with toothpick, but try not to poke cranberries. Let stand 10 minutes and remove from pan. Cool on rack; wrap and serve the next day.

Date LOAF

1 teaspoon baking soda
1 cup chopped dates
1 cup boiling water
1 teaspoon butter
1 cup sugar

1 teaspoon vanilla
1 egg
2 cups flour
1 teaspoon baking powder
½ cup chopped walnuts

Sprinkle soda on dates; add boiling water and let stand. When cool, add butter, sugar, vanilla, beaten egg, then dry ingredients. Bake in 325° oven for 1 hour or until a toothpick comes out clean when poked into loaf.

Gumdrop LOAF

½ cup butter
2 eggs
1 cup sugar
1 cup milk
1 teaspoon vanilla
1 teaspoon allspice
2 cups flour

2 teaspoons baking powder
¼ teaspoon salt
1 teaspoon cinnamon
1 pound baking-type gumdrops
1 pound raisins
1 cup walnuts

Cream butter and eggs; add sugar, milk, and vanilla. Add dry ingredients. Pour into two 9x5-inch loaf pans, greased and lined with waxed paper. Bake at 350° for 1 hour.

Poppyseed LOAF

Batter:

- ¼ cup poppyseeds
- ¾ cup milk
- ½ cup butter or margarine
- ¾ cup sugar
- 2 eggs
- 1 teaspoon lemon juice
- 2 cups flour
- 2½ teaspoons baking powder
- Pinch salt
- ½ cup maraschino cherries, well drained and halved

Glaze:

- 5 tablespoons brown sugar
- 2 tablespoons cream or milk
- 1 tablespoon butter or margarine
- 1–2 tablespoons crushed nuts

Put poppyseeds and milk in small bowl. Let stand for 30 minutes. Combine butter, sugar, and 1 egg in mixing bowl. Beat well. Add second egg and lemon juice. Beat until smooth. Stir in poppyseed mixture. Measure flour, baking powder, and salt together in small bowl. Mix well. Stir into batter until just moistened. Fold in cherries. Pour into greased loaf pan. Bake in 350° oven for 1 hour. Mix and pour glaze over top (optional).

Lemon LOAF

½ cup butter
1 cup sugar
2 eggs, well beaten
½ cup milk
Rind of 1 lemon

¼ teaspoon salt
1½ cups flour
1 teaspoon baking powder
1½ cups glazed cherries,
    dredged in flour

Topping:
Juice of 1 lemon

¼ cup sugar

Cream butter; add sugar and cream until light. Add eggs, mixing well. Add milk and stir. Add rind. Sift together salt, flour, and baking powder and add to mixture. Fold in cherries. Bake in an ungreased loaf pan at 350° for approximately 1 hour. Mix topping and pour over top of loaf while loaf is still hot.

Paradise LOAF

²/₃ cup butter
1 cup sugar
3 eggs
3 cups flour
¹/₄ teaspoon salt
1 teaspoon baking powder

¹/₂ cup milk
1 pound raisins
2 rings glazed pineapple, diced
¹/₂ cup glazed cherries, cut in half
1 teaspoon rum flavoring

Cream butter; add sugar and then the eggs one at a time, beating well. Sift dry ingredients and add to mixture alternately with milk. Blend the fruit together and fold into mixture, along with flavoring. Pour into greased loaf pan and bake at 325° for approximately 1 hour.

PIES

After Jesus was born in Bethlehem in Judea,

during the time of King Herod,

Magi from the east came to Jerusalem and asked,

"Where is the one who has been born king of the Jews?

We saw his star in the east and have come to worship him."

MATTHEW 2:1–2

ANY *Fruit* OR *Berry* PIE

Fruit or berries, fresh or frozen
(enough to fill the pie shell)
¾ cup sugar
2 cups water
2 tablespoons cornstarch

Pinch salt
1 small package jelly powder,
same flavor as the fruit
1 baked pie shell, cooled
1 small container whipped cream

Drain berries, pat dry, and sprinkle with sugar. Set aside. Mix water, cornstarch, and salt. Bring to a boil; add jelly powder and mix until dissolved. Continue to boil until syrupy. Remove from heat and let cool until the right consistency to add the fruit or berries, partially set enough to mix smoothly and not have the fruit sink. It also must be cool enough so as not to cook the fruit or berries. Pour into baked pie shell. Chill completely. Top with whipped cream. Serve.

Chocolate DREAM PIE

2 envelopes Dream Whip
1 ¾ cups milk
2 packages chocolate instant pudding (4-serving size)
1 9-inch pie shell, baked and cooled (or 1 9-inch graham
    cracker crumb crust)

Prepare dessert topping mix as directed on package, using large mixer bowl. Add milk and pudding mix. Blend, then beat on high speed for 2 minutes, scraping bowl occasionally. Spoon into pie shell. Chill for 3 hours.

Banana Butterscotch PIE

2 cups milk
1/3 cup flour
3/4 cup brown sugar
1/2 teaspoon salt
3 egg yolks, beaten

2 tablespoons butter
1/2 teaspoon vanilla
1 baked pie shell, cooled
2 large bananas
Sweetened whipped cream

Heat milk slowly in double boiler or microwave. Combine with dry ingredients and cook until thick, stirring frequently with a whisk. Stir small amount into beaten egg yolks, return to main mixture, and continue cooking 2 minutes longer. Remove from heat and beat in butter and vanilla. Cool slightly. Pour small amount over bottom of pie shell. Slice one banana over top. Pour in remaining filling. Chill. Serve with whipped cream and garnish with bananas.

French Apple PIE (TORTE)

Base:
- 1 1/3 cups flour
- 3 tablespoons icing sugar
- 2/3 cup butter at room temperature

Filling:
- 3/4 cup sugar
- 1/4 teaspoon salt
- 2 tablespoons flour
- 1/2 teaspoon cinnamon
- 2 tablespoons butter at room temperature
- 7 thinly sliced apples

Topping:
- 1 1/4 cups flour
- 1/2 cup packed brown sugar
- 1/3 cup butter, room temperature

For pastry combine flour and icing sugar; cut in butter until crumbly. Press dough over bottom and 2 inches up sides of 9-inch spring form pan. Chill.

For filling combine dry ingredients and cut in butter. Add apples; toss to coat. Place apple mix in prepared crust.

For topping combine flour and brown sugar in bowl. Cut in butter. Squeeze handfuls of topping into firm chunks; break chunks apart into smaller pieces. Sprinkle over apples.

Bake at 350° for 60–75 minutes or until apples are done. Cover loosely with foil if browning too quickly. Cool completely.

Impossible CHERRY PIE

Crust:

1 cup milk

¼ teaspoon almond extract

½ cup Bisquik

2 tablespoons butter or margarine

2 eggs

¼ cup sugar

Filling:

1 21-ounce can cherry pie filling

Streusel Topping:

2 tablespoons firm butter or margarine

½ cup brown sugar

½ cup Bisquik

½ teaspoon cinnamon

In blender, mix all ingredients of crust together for 15 seconds on high or 1 minute on high speed of electric hand mixer. Pour into greased 10-inch pie plate. Pour in cherry pie filling. Bake 25 minutes at 350°. While this is baking, make Streusel Topping by cutting butter into the dry ingredients until crumbly. When pie comes out of the oven, sprinkle the Streusel Topping on top and put it back in the oven until brown, about 10 minutes. Cool and serve. Refrigerate any uneaten portion.

Blueberry CREAM PIE

2 cups milk
1 tablespoon butter
2 tablespoons lemon juice, divided
1 teaspoon vanilla
2 eggs, beaten
¼ cup hot water

¾ cup sugar, divided
2 cups blueberries, drained if frozen
4½ tablespoons cornstarch
1 baked pie shell, cooled
1 pint whipping cream, whipped

Heat milk gently; add butter, 1 tablespoon lemon juice and 1 teaspoon vanilla. Bring to boil then add beaten eggs; boil until thickened. Cool and pour into pie shell. Add 1 tablespoon lemon juice, water, and ¼ cup sugar to blueberries. Bring to a boil and thicken with 1½ tablespoons cornstarch mixed in just enough water so it doesn't make lumps when added to blueberry mixture. Cool; pour on top of pie. Top with whipped cream. Garnish with a few leftover blueberries.

Pecan PIE

1 shell of your favorite pastry, uncooked
1 cup pecans
3 eggs
$\frac{1}{2}$ cup sugar

1 cup corn syrup
$\frac{1}{8}$ teaspoon salt
1 teaspoon vanilla
$\frac{1}{4}$ cup butter, melted

Line pie plate with pastry. Spread pecans on top. Set aside. Beat eggs; add sugar, syrup, salt, vanilla, and melted butter. Pour over top of pecans. Bake at 350° for 50–60 minutes.

Peach PIE

1½ cups flour
½ cup margarine
Pinch of salt

1 15-ounce can peaches, halved
1 cup sugar
½ teaspoon cinnamon

Mix flour, margarine, and salt together; put into an 8x8-inch cake pan and flatten with a spoon. Drain can of peaches, saving ½ cup of the juice. Place peaches on top of crust. Mix sugar and cinnamon together then sprinkle over peaches. Bake in a 350° oven for 20 minutes. Remove from oven and let stand while you mix:

1 egg
½ cup peach juice

1 cup evaporated milk

Pour mixture on top of peaches and bake for another 30 minutes at 375°, until custard is set.

Pumpkin ICE CREAM PIE

1½ cups gingersnap crumbs
⅓ cup sugar
⅓ cup melted butter
1 envelope unflavored gelatin
¼ cup cold water
¾ cup canned pumpkin

¾ teaspoon salt
2¼ teaspoons pumpkin pie spice
1½ teaspoons vanilla
6 cups vanilla ice cream, softened
Prepared pie shell

Combine gingersnap crumbs, sugar, and butter; mix well. Press into a 9-inch pie plate. Refrigerate until needed. In a saucepan, soften gelatin in cold water. Stir in pumpkin, salt, and pie spice. Stir over low heat until gelatin is dissolved. Add vanilla and cool to room temperature. Fold ice cream into mixture. Pour into prepared pie shell. If desired, sprinkle with additional gingersnap crumbs. Freeze until firm. Remove from freezer 10 minutes before serving.

Perfect LEMON PIE

Filling:

7 tablespoons cornstarch

1 ½ cups sugar

½ teaspoon salt

2 cups boiling water

3 egg yolks

¼ cup lemon juice

2 tablespoons butter

2 tablespoons grated lemon peel

1 baked pastry shell

Meringue:

3 egg whites

6 tablespoons sugar

Pinch cream of tartar

Pinch salt

Combine cornstarch, sugar, and salt. Add water. Cook until thick, stirring constantly. Beat egg yolks slightly. Add a little hot water mixture; stir and pour all back into main mixture. Cook 2 minutes, stirring constantly. Remove from heat and stir in lemon juice, butter, and lemon rind. Cool to room temperature without stirring. Pour into pastry shell. To make meringue, beat 3 egg whites until it makes fine foam mounds. Add 6 tablespoons sugar, 1 tablespoon at a time. Beat after each addition; at last addition, add cream of tartar and salt. Beat until consistency is right. Spread on filling, and bake at 350° for 15 minutes or until slightly golden.

Raisin AND *Rhubarb* PIE

1 cup rhubarb, fresh or frozen
1 cup raisins
1 cup sugar

1 lemon, juice and grated rind
1 egg
1 premade crust, fresh or frozen

If rhubarb is fresh, peel and cut into ½-inch pieces. Cover with boiling water, let stand 5 minutes, and drain. Wash raisins and mix with rhubarb. Add other ingredients. Pour into pie shell. Bake 30–35 minutes at 325° or until golden brown.

SLICES & SQUARES

When they saw the star, they were overjoyed.
On coming to the house, they saw the child with his mother Mary,
and they bowed down and worshiped him.
Then they opened their treasures and presented him
with gifts of gold and of incense and of myrrh.

MATTHEW 2:10–11

Apricot SQUARES

9 apricots, halved and pitted
1 cup butter or margarine, divided
1/3 cup firmly packed brown sugar
9 maraschino cherries
1 cup sugar
2 large eggs

2 cups cake flour, divided
2 teaspoons baking powder
1/2 teaspoon salt
1 teaspoon grated lemon rind
2/3 cup milk

Cut each apricot half into four slices. Melt ¼ cup butter and pour into bottom of 9-inch square pan. Sprinkle brown sugar evenly over butter. Arrange cherries and half the apricot slices in sugar mixture. Chop remaining apricot slices; set aside. Beat sugar, eggs, and remaining ¾ cup butter. Add in 1 cup of the flour, baking powder, salt, and lemon rind. Gradually beat in remaining flour alternately with milk until batter is smooth. Stir in reserved chopped apricots. Carefully spoon batter over apricots in pan. Bake at 350° for 45–50 minutes or until cake springs back when top is lightly touched with finger. Remove from oven and place serving plate facedown over cake. Turn upside down to unmold. Cut into squares. Serve warm or at room temperature. Makes 9 squares.

Cherry Banana SLICE

10 ounces margarine
6 ounces caster sugar
3 large eggs
6 ounces self-rising flour
1 teaspoon baking powder

2 bananas, peeled and mashed
  (separately)
1 lemon, rind and juice, divided
8 ounces sifted icing sugar
4 glacé cherries, halved

Beat 6 ounces margarine with sugar, eggs, flour, and baking powder. Add 1 banana, lemon rind, and 1 tablespoon juice and beat until smooth. Bake in greased 9-inch square pan at 375° for 50 minutes. Cool. Set aside. Mix remaining banana with 1 teaspoon lemon juice. Set aside. Cream rest of margarine with icing sugar and remaining lemon juice. Reserve half; mix chopped banana into one half. Trim edges of the cake and cut in half; sandwich halves together with banana icing. Spread a third of the remaining icing over top of cake. Put remaining icing in a piping bag fitted with a star nozzle. Pipe swirls round top of cake, then decorate with halved cherries.

Almond SQUARES

Base:

1 ½ cups flour
½ cup butter

2 tablespoons icing sugar

Bend and press into a 9-inch square pan. Bake for 10 minutes at 350°.

Filling:

4 tablespoons butter
1 cup brown sugar
¼ cup sour cream

1 ½ cups slivered almonds
3 teaspoons vanilla

Boil first 4 ingredients for 3 minutes. Add slivered almonds. Spread over base and bake for 10 minutes at 350°.

Cherry CHA-CHA

Crust:

   ½ cup butter
   ¼ cup sugar

2 cups graham wafer crumbs

Melt butter. Stir in sugar and crumbs. Save ⅓ for topping. Press into a greased 9x13-inch pan. Bake at 350° for 10 minutes. Cool.

Filling:

   2 cups whipping cream
   4 cups small marshmallows

1 19-ounce can cherry pie filling

Whip cream and fold in marshmallows. Spread half on crust. Spoon pie filling on top and smooth. Spread other half of cream mixture on top of pie filling. Sprinkle crumbs on top. Chill for several hours. Cut into 12 pieces.

Cherry SLICE

1 cup soft butter or margarine
1½ cups sugar
4 eggs
1 teaspoon vanilla

2 teaspoons almond flavoring
3 cups flour
1 can cherry pie filling

Cream butter and sugar. Add 1 egg at a time, mixing well after each addition. Add flavorings. Add flour, 1 cup at a time, mixing well. Batter will be very soft; do not add more flour. Spread ⅔ of the batter in bottom of greased 15x10-inch jelly roll pan. Spread on can of pie filling (in such a way that you will leave small spaces with no pie filling). Spread on remaining ⅓ of batter. Bake at 350° for 30–40 minutes, or until golden. Sprinkle with icing sugar when cool.

Cherry SNACK

1 cup flour
½ cup butter
1 tablespoon brown sugar
½ cup glazed cherries
1½ cups brown sugar
2 eggs
1 cup chopped walnuts
½ cup shredded coconut

2 tablespoons flour
Pinch salt
1 teaspoon baking powder
1½ cups icing sugar
1 tablespoon butter
1 teaspoon vanilla
Milk to moisten

Mix flour, butter, and 1 tablespoon brown sugar; bake in 8x11-inch pan at 350° for approximately 10 minutes, until golden brown. Set some cherries aside and mix remaining sugar, eggs, fruit, nuts, coconut, flour, salt, and baking powder. Pour over base and bake at 300° for 20–30 minutes, until brown. Cool. Mix icing sugar, butter, vanilla, and enough milk to make into a nice icing. Spread on cooled cake and decorate with pieces of cherries.

Chewy Chocolate BARS

1 package chocolate chips
1 can Eagle condensed milk
¾ cup butter, softened
1¼ cups packed brown sugar

2 eggs
1½ cups flour
¾ cup rolled oats
½ teaspoon salt

Melt chocolate chips with milk. Cream butter and brown sugar until soft; beat in eggs. Blend in flour, rolled oats, and salt. Spread half of mixture in greased 13x9-inch pan. Spread chocolate mixture base. Spread remaining dough over chocolate layer. Bake at 350° for 35 minutes. Cool and cut into bars. Makes about 30 bars.

Coffee Chocolate DESSERT

Graham cracker squares (not crumbs)
1 pint whipping cream (2 cups)
½ cup icing sugar
4 tablespoons liquid chocolate
    sundae topping

1 tablespoon instant dry coffee
Chocolate decoration—
    shaved chocolate or
    chocolate sprinkles

Place layer of graham crackers in 9x9-inch pan. Whip cream; add next 3 ingredients. Place ⅓ of mixture on crackers. Repeat with crackers then add second ⅓ of the mixture, top with crackers, then last ⅓ of the mixture. Sprinkle top with chocolate decoration.

Danish APPLE BARS

2½ cups flour
1 teaspoon salt
1 cup shortening
1 egg, separated
Milk
1 cup crushed cornflakes

4 cups diced and peeled apples
1 cup sugar
1 teaspoon cinnamon
1 cup icing sugar
2 tablespoons water
1 teaspoon vanilla

Sift the flour and salt. Cut in shortening until coarse. Set egg white aside. Beat egg yolk slightly. Add enough milk to the egg yolk to make ⅔ cup. Slowly add egg/milk mixture to flour mixture until it resembles pie dough. Divide dough in half. Roll one portion into rectangle to fit jelly roll pan and bring up on sides. Sprinkle crushed cornflakes on top of crust. Set aside. Sprinkle apples with sugar and cinnamon, then spread apples over the cornflakes. Roll out remaining dough to fit over apples. Moisten edges with milk and seal. Beat egg white until stiff. Brush over top crust. Bake at 350° for approximately 1 hour. Combine icing sugar, water, and vanilla. Spread over top while still warm.

Dream BARS

Base:

1½ cups flour   ½ cup firmly packed brown sugar
½ cup butter, softened

Blend the above ingredients until crumbly. Press into an ungreased 13x9-inch baking pan. Bake at 350° for 12 minutes.

Filling:

3 eggs   ¼ cup flour
1½ cups firmly packed brown sugar   1 teaspoon baking powder
Pinch salt   1 teaspoon vanilla
1½ cups shredded unsweetened   1 cup chopped walnuts
   coconut

Beat eggs and 1½ cups brown sugar for 2 minutes at highest speed of an electric mixer. Blend in remaining ingredients at low speed. Pour and spread over partially baked crust. Bake at 350° for 20–30 minutes, until deep golden brown. Cool. Cut into bars using a knife dipped in hot water.

Dreamy APRICOT SQUARES

1 cup crushed graham wafer crumbs	2 eggs
1 cup sifted all-purpose flour	1 cup brown sugar
1 cup shredded coconut	1 teaspoon lemon juice
½ teaspoon salt	⅓ cup sifted flour
1 cup melted butter	½ teaspoon baking powder
1 cup dried apricots	¼ teaspoon salt

Combine crumbs, flour, coconut, and salt. Add melted butter and mix. Reserve 1 cup for topping. Pack remainder in 9x9-inch pan. Bake for 10 minutes at 350°. Chop apricots and cover with water. Simmer until tender, approximately 15 minutes, and drain. Beat eggs until light and add brown sugar and lemon juice. Stir in dry ingredients and spread over bottom. Layer and sprinkle with reserved cup for topping. Bake for 30–35 minutes at 350°. Cool and cut into squares.

Frosted OATMEAL SQUARES

2 cups quick oats
1/2 cup firmly packed brown sugar
1/2 cup softened butter or margarine
1/4 cup light corn syrup
3 ounces (1/2 cup) semisweet chocolate chips
1/3 cup chunky peanut butter

Mix oats, brown sugar, butter, and corn syrup. Press mixture evenly in a
12x8-inch glass baking dish and microwave on high for 3 1/2–4 minutes or until
bubbly over entire top. Cool. Melt chocolate and peanut butter for approximately 1 minute, stirring halfway through. Mix until smooth. Spread on cooled
oatmeal mixture. Chill and cut into squares.

 *Flaky* PINEAPPLE SQUARES

Crust:

    4 cups flour   1 cup sour cream
    1 pound butter

    Mix flour and butter. Add sour cream and refrigerate for 2 hours.

Filling:

    2 tins crushed pineapple, including juice   1 cup sugar
    3–4 tablespoons cornstarch

Topping:

    Icing sugar

Combine the above filling mix and cook until thickened. Let cool. Roll half the dough onto jelly-roll pan. Spread with cooled filling. Top with remaining dough. Pierce top of dough with fork. Bake at 325° for approximately 50 minutes. Cool and sprinkle with icing sugar.

GRAHAM *Napoleons*

57–60 graham wafers, whole
2 small packages cream cheese
2 packages instant vanilla pudding mix
4 cups cold milk
½ cup whipping cream, whipped
1 envelope unflavored gelatin

¼ cup water
1 cup fresh or frozen strawberries, chopped
1 cup icing sugar
2 tablespoons milk
2 tablespoons strawberry jam, melted

Line bottom of 13x9-inch pan with wafers to cover bottom of pan. Beat 4 cups milk with pudding mix for 2 minutes. Set aside.

Beat cream cheese until fluffy, fold into pudding mix, then fold in whipped cream. Take $3\frac{1}{2}$ cups of this mixture and set aside. Soften gelatin in $\frac{1}{4}$ cup water for 5 minutes. Dissolve over low heat, stirring constantly. Mix gelatin into strawberries and fold into remaining pudding mixture. Pour strawberry mixture evenly into prepared pan. Top with another layer of wafers, then pour reserved vanilla cream mixture over this. Top with remaining wafers and refrigerate until set. Top with glaze made from icing sugar and 2 tablespoons milk. Do not allow icing to set. While the icing is still drippy, pipe or drizzle straight lines of melted jam over the icing. Draw the tip of a knife or a toothpick through the lines to make a pleasing pattern. Makes 18 bars.

 *Mint* SWIRL BARS

Bars:

- 1 3-ounce package cream cheese
- ¼ cup butter (do not use margarine)
- ¾ cup sugar
- 2 eggs
- ⅔ cup flour
- ½ teaspoon baking powder
- ½ teaspoon salt
- ⅓ cup chopped walnuts
- 1 1-ounce square semisweet chocolate, melted
- ½ teaspoon peppermint extract
- 2–3 drops green food coloring

Glaze:

- 1 1-ounce square semisweet chocolate
- 1 tablespoon butter
- 1 cup icing sugar
- ½ teaspoon vanilla
- 2–3 tablespoons boiling water

Beat cream cheese, butter, and sugar. Add eggs, one at a time, beating well after each addition. Combine flour, powder, and salt; mix well. Transfer half of the batter to another bowl; set aside. To half of mixture, stir in nuts and chocolate. Spread in greased 9-inch square pan. To other half, stir in peppermint extract and food coloring. Spoon over chocolate layer and cut with a knife to swirl. Bake at 350° for 15–20 minutes until toothpick comes out clean. Cool on wire rack. Melt chocolate and butter, remove from heat, then stir in icing sugar, vanilla, and enough water to achieve a glaze consistency. Pour over cooled cake and spread evenly. Cut into bars. Makes 2 dozen.

Frosted PEANUT SQUARES

½ cup firmly packed brown sugar
½ cup peanut butter
½ cup corn syrup
1 cup roughly chopped peanuts
4 cups cornflakes
1 cup melted chocolate chips

Combine brown sugar, peanut butter, and corn syrup in large saucepan. Cook over medium heat until mixture starts to bubble, stirring constantly. Remove from heat; stir in peanuts and cornflakes, using two forks to mix thoroughly. Press warm mixture evenly and firmly into buttered 13x9-inch rectangular pan. Spread roughly with melted chocolate chips and cool. Cut into squares when firm. Yield: 24 2-inch squares.

Marshmallow DREAM SQUARES

½ package graham wafers, crushed
⅓ package miniature marshmallows
½ cup chopped dates
¼ cup fine coconut or nuts

½ cup melted butter
½ cup brown sugar
1 egg

Mix together graham wafers, marshmallows, dates, and coconut/nuts. Melt butter and brown sugar together. Beat in egg and mix. Combine with rest of mixed ingredients. Pack into buttered pan. Refrigerate. Cover with your favorite butter icing, if desired.

Peanut Butter BARS

½ cup sugar
½ cup light corn syrup
1 cup peanut butter
1 teaspoon vanilla
2 cups cornflake cereal
1 cup Rice Krispies cereal
⅓ cup brown sugar
¼ cup cream

Heat sugar and corn syrup until sugar melts. Add peanut butter and vanilla. Mix and add cereals. Heat again and pack into a greased 9x9-inch pan. Boil brown sugar and cream together for 2 minutes (will be thin). Pour on cake. Allow to set when cool.

Penuche SQUARES

Base:

½ cup butter	1 teaspoon vanilla
½ cup sugar	1 cup cake flour
2 egg yolks	1 teaspoon baking powder

Topping:

2 egg whites	1 cup walnuts
1 cup brown sugar	

Cream butter and sugar together. Add egg yolks and vanilla and then dry ingredients. Press into 9x9-inch greased pan. Set aside. Beat egg whites until stiff, but not dry, and gradually add brown sugar. Fold in walnuts. Bake at 325° for approximately 35 minutes.

Rainbow BARS

Base:

½ cup butter

2 cups flour

2 tablespoons sugar

Mix well. Spread in 9x12-inch pan. Bake for 15 minutes at 350°.

Filling:

3 tablespoons cornstarch

½ cup maraschino cherries, cut up

1 teaspoon almond flavoring

1 tin crushed pineapple, with juice

½ cup sugar

Mix the cornstarch with cherry juice, to make a paste, and mix all filling ingredients. Cook about 15 minutes until thick. Pour on top of base while both are still hot.

Topping:

3 egg whites

1 teaspoon vanilla

Coconut (optional)

3 tablespoons sugar

Pinch salt

Beat well and spread on cake. Sprinkle with coconut, if desired, and bake at 350° until topping is brown.

Smoothie SQUARES

1 package graham wafers (whole)
1 large package vanilla pudding
     (cooked, not instant)
2 cups milk
1½ cups whipping cream

1 cup icing sugar
1 tablespoon butter
1–2 tablespoons milk
1 square semisweet chocolate

Line a 9x13-inch pan with graham wafers. Cook vanilla pudding with milk
and spread over wafers. Cool. Whip cream and spread over pudding. Cover with
graham wafers. Prepare icing by beating icing sugar, butter, and enough milk to
make the texture thin but not too liquidy. Glaze over top layer of graham wafers.
Swirl in melted chocolate.

SNACKS

"For God so loved the world
that he gave his one and only Son,
that whoever believes in him shall not perish
but have eternal life."

JOHN 3:16

 Apple PUFFS

Puffs:

¼ cup melted butter
½ cup sugar
½ cup milk
1 egg, slightly beaten
1½ cups flour

1 tablespoon baking powder
Pinch salt
½ teaspoon cinnamon
1 cup apples, peeled and
    finely chopped

Topping:

¼ cup sugar
½ teaspoon cinnamon

¼ cup finely chopped walnuts
1 apple, peeled and thinly sliced

Combine butter and sugar. Stir in milk and egg. Add flour, baking powder, salt, and cinnamon. Stir just enough to mix. Fold in chopped apples. Spoon batter into greased muffin cups. Mix sugar, cinnamon, and walnuts and sprinkle evenly over muffins, then top each with an apple slice. Bake at 350° for 20 minutes.

Caramel SHORTBREAD

Base:

1 cup butter	¼ teaspoon salt
½ cup sifted icing sugar	1¼ cups flour

Beat butter, sugar, and salt until fluffy. Add flour. Spread in a greased 9-inch pan. Bake at 350° for 30 minutes.

Topping:

½ cup butter	1 teaspoon vanilla
1 can sweetened condensed milk	2 squares semisweet chocolate,
3 tablespoons honey	melted

Melt butter in microwave. Stir in milk and honey. Cook on high for 6–8 minutes until caramel color, stirring after each minute. Add vanilla. Spread over shortbread, drizzle with melted chocolate, and chill until firm.

Christmas SHORTBREAD

1 cup butter
¼ cup sugar
2 cups flour
1½ cups coconut
⅔ cup red or green cherries

¼ cup raisins or currants
⅓ cup chopped walnuts or almonds
1 cup Eagle Brand canned milk
Icing sugar

Cream butter and sugar. Blend in flour until mixture resembles coarse crumbs. Pat into greased 9-inch square pan. Bake at 350° for 20 minutes. Combine remaining ingredients. Spread over shortbread and bake an additional 35 minutes or until golden brown. Cool and cut into bars. Dust with icing sugar.

Cocoa KRISPIE ROLL

³/₄ cup corn syrup
³/₄ cup sugar
³/₄ cup peanut butter
2 tablespoons butter
4¹/₂ cups Rice Krispies cereal

¹/₃ cup butter
2 tablespoons milk
1¹/₂ cups icing sugar
²/₃ cup cocoa

Cook corn syrup and sugar until sugar dissolves and mixture bubbles. Remove from heat; blend in peanut butter and 2 tablespoons butter. Add Rice Krispies; stir until well coated. Press firmly into buttered 15x10-inch jelly-roll pan or cookie sheet. Melt ¹/₃ cup butter with milk over low heat. Remove from heat; sift in icing sugar and cocoa. Blend thoroughly. Remove Rice Krispies from pan; spread evenly with cocoa mix. Starting at short end roll up to form a log. Wrap in greased waxed paper; refrigerate until firm. Remove 30 minutes before serving. Cut into ¹/₂-inch slices.

Cranberry, Chocolate, Orange ROUNDS

2 cups raw cranberries, chopped
½ cup sugar
3½ cups flour
1½ cups sugar
1 teaspoon baking powder
1 teaspoon baking soda
1 teaspoon salt

2 eggs
1½ cups orange juice
¼ cup oil
1 tablespoon grated orange rind
2 cups semisweet chocolate chips
1 cup chopped nuts

Combine cranberries and ½ cup sugar and set aside. Combine 1½ cups sugar and balance of dry ingredients. Beat eggs, juice, oil, and rind together and add to dry ingredients; stir just until moistened. Fold in cranberries, chocolate chips, and nuts. Divide batter into 8 or 9 well-greased 10-ounce soup cans. Fill just over half full and bake at 350° for 35–40 minutes or until done. Cool 10 minutes then run blade of thin knife around edges of tin to loosen. Turn out on rack to cool completely. Wrap and store overnight before slicing or freeze for later use.

Almond ROCA

1 tablespoon corn syrup
¼ cup sugar
1 cup butter

¼ cup water
1¼ cups toasted slivered almonds
1 6-ounce package chocolate chips

In a large, heavy saucepan, gently boil syrup, sugar, butter, and water until it reaches the "hard crack" stage on candy thermometer (300F/150C). Do not stir! This takes about 10 minutes. To be sure, drop a small amount of the mixture into cold water to see if it turns brittle. Remove from heat and add almonds. Spread onto an ungreased cookie sheet. Sprinkle with chocolate chips while still hot and spread evenly when melted. Cool in fridge or freezer. Break into bite-size pieces. Note: This recipe does not double.

Five-minute NEVER-FAIL FUDGE

²/₃ cup evaporated milk	16 large marshmallows, cut up
1 ⅓ cups sugar	1 ½ cups semisweet chocolate chips
¼ teaspoon salt	1 teaspoon vanilla
¼ cup butter	1 cup broken walnuts

Mix together milk, sugar, salt, butter, and marshmallows and bring to a boil, stirring constantly. Boil 5 minutes. Remove from heat. Add chocolate and stir until melted. Stir in vanilla and walnuts. Spread in buttered 8-inch square pan. Cool until firm.

Mocha Meringue KISSES

These are heart smart!

3 egg whites
¼ teaspoon cream of tartar
⅔ cup sugar
½ teaspoon vanilla

2 teaspoons cornstarch
1 tablespoon crushed instant coffee
¼ cup finely chopped almonds

Beat egg whites with cream of tartar until frothy; gradually add ⅓ cup sugar and beat until stiff. Add vanilla. Mix ⅓ cup with cornstarch, coffee powder, and nuts. Fold in egg whites. Spoon into parchment paper-lined baking sheets. Bake in preheated 300° oven for 30 minutes. Turn off oven. Allow these to cool in oven. Tops should be dry and slightly browned. Variation: Use cocoa powder instead of instant coffee.

Peanut Butter LOGS

1 cup peanut butter
2 cups icing sugar
1 cup chopped walnuts

1 cup chopped dates
4 squares semisweet chocolate, melted
Shredded coconut

Mix like a pastry and roll dough into a small log. Dip or roll in chocolate and roll in coconut. If dough is too stiff to roll, add a little coffee or milk.

Peanut Mallow TREATS

¼ cup butter or margarine
6 cups mini marshmallows
½ cup smooth or crunchy
   peanut butter

4 cups Honey Bunches of
   Oats cereal
1 cup semisweet chocolate chips

Melt butter and marshmallows. Stir until smooth. Stir in peanut butter and cereal. Add chips. Roll into balls and place on greased baking sheet. Chill. Makes 36.

Raspberry ROLL

Syrup:

1 cup brown sugar

1 cup water

Boil for 10 minutes. Set aside.

Biscuit dough:

2 cups flour

4 teaspoons baking powder

½ cup milk

4 tablespoons shortening

1 teaspoon salt

Butter for spreading

1 package frozen raspberries, drained and patted dry

Make biscuit dough and roll ½–inch thick. Spread with raspberries. Roll like a jelly-roll. Cut into 1½–inch slices. Lightly butter each slice and cover with syrup. Bake at 350° for 25–30 minutes.

Snowcup BROWNIES

½ cup flour
½ teaspoon salt
½ cup butter or margarine
1 cup sugar
2 eggs
1 teaspoon vanilla

2 squares unsweetened
  chocolate, melted
1 cup quick rolled oats
½ cup chopped walnuts
Confectioners' sugar

Mix flour and salt; add butter, sugar, eggs, vanilla, and chocolate. Beat until smooth, about 2 minutes. Add rolled oats and walnuts. Spread in a greased 8x8-inch pan. Bake at 350° for 25 minutes. Cool in pan. Cut into squares and sprinkle with confectioners' sugar. Makes 16.